AF595924

Riding Life's Rollercoaster without Freaking Out

Dr. MICHAEL BERNARD
and HELEN JAMES

Published by Wilkinson Publishing Pty Ltd
ACN 006 042 173
PO Box 24135, Melbourne, VIC 3001, Australia.
Ph: +61 3 9654 5446
enquiries@wilkinsonpublishing.com.au
www.wilkinsonpublishing.com.au

WilkinsonPublishing

wilkinsonpublishinghouse

Title: AHA! Moments
ISBN: 9781921804588
A catalogue record of this book is available from the National Library of Australia.

Illustrations by Helen James.
Printed and bound in China through Asia Pacific Offset.

INTRODUCTION

If you feel like you're on a rollercoaster hanging on for dear life, you're not alone. Today's world is more stressful than ever - we're all on 24/7, often struggling to keep from falling off.

Perhaps that's the very reason this book found its way into your hands. You're seeking fresh ideas to navigate life's chaos without losing yourself in the process.

In our book, you'll discover proven insights developed by many of the world's greatest thought leaders* - called *AHA! Moments*. They enable us to stay calm, solve problems and thrive despite the pandemonium of life. We created a fictional character, Sunny, to communicate different *AHA! Moments*.

The foundation of wellbeing is clear. It is the way we see things, our individual perspective. This book's focus is on helping all of us adopt open, flexible and sensible ways to see and interpret ourselves, others and the world. This leads to a greater sense of optimism and happiness.

And what's great about this book is that it's not like traditional, word-heavy, self-help books. Every page presents one illustration which demonstrates the thought-provoking insights on the adjoining page.

We wrote this book because we share an unwavering passion for helping people to live their lives with less stress and more joy. Our aim was to make this book thought-provoking and enjoyable.

Most importantly, we hope it will give you ideas you can put into practice right away that will make an immediate difference to your life.

Michael and Helen

*Specialists in the fields of brain neuroscience, positive psychology, rational-emotive, cognitive-behaviour therapy, peak performance, personal growth and flourishing. Their work provides many of the *AHA! Moments* in this book. They include Aaron Beck, Buddha, Andrew Bustamonte, Deepak Chopra, Susan David, Albert Ellis, Epictetus, Barbara Frederickson, Stephen Hayes, Arianna Huffington, Susan Jeffers, Katie Ledecky, Abraham Maslow, Reinhold Niebuhr, Martin Seligman, William Shakespeare, Melanie Shmois, Jim VandeHei (and we provide some too!).

ABOUT THE AUTHORS

Dr Michael Bernard, PhD, is an international consultant, former University of Melbourne Professor and currently an Emeritus Professor at California State University, Long Beach. He founded You Can Do It! Education, Australia's first K-12 social-emotional learning program used in 5,000+ schools globally. He has worked as a consultant school psychologist helping families and schools address the educational and mental health needs of school-age children. Michael is the author of the *Survey of Student Wellbeing* (ACER) completed by 500,000+ students. Michael was Collingwood Football Club's first sport psychologist and co-founded the Australian Institute for Rational Emotive Therapy. He has authored/edited 50+ books on rational-emotive behavior therapy, peak performance, procrastination and stress management.

Helen James has a Master of Arts Degree in Clinical Psychology from the University of Melbourne and prior to this she studied Graphic Design at the Swinburne College of Technology (now Swinburne University), Melbourne. She has had a multifaceted career as a Graphic Designer and Illustrator, Clinical Psychologist, Management/Organization Development Consultant, Corporate Executive and Owner/Chief Designer of an import/wholesale giftware company in USA.

Helen's current focus is combining her love of creating art and interest in wellbeing/personal development with producing inspirational, illustrated, thought-provoking books. Her previous published work in this genre is *PUG: How to Be the Best You* (2017). Exisle Publishing.

DEDICATION

MICHAEL

To Patricia, Jonathon, and Alexandra -
your love is my greatest AHA! moment.

HELEN

A big thank you to my partner Gerard Dillon who introduced me to Michael and also for his unwavering support during this creative journey. And to my loving family and friends who are always there for me.

Meet Sunny.
Sunny is just like you and me.
Some days life is bathed
in sunshine -
things are going well and
Sunny is happy and content.

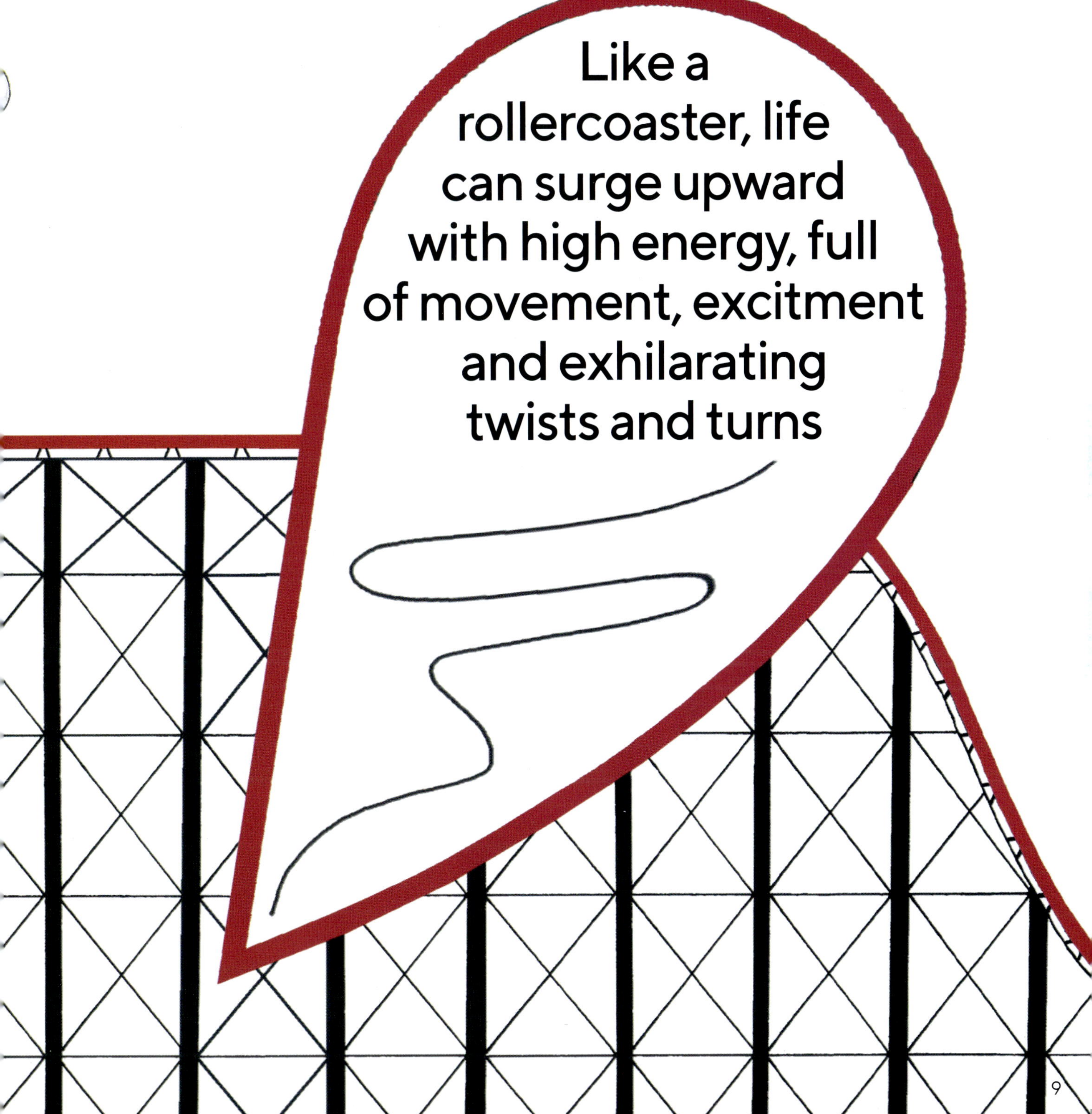
Like a
rollercoaster, life
can surge upward
with high energy, full
of movement, excitment
and exhilarating
twists and turns

There are also days
when Sunny's life is cloaked
in shadows, full of shade.
THINGS SEEM TO
FALL APART.

THE ROLLER COASTER CAN DROP -

exhaustion, negativity and sadness taking hold.

BEST

You can be overloaded with not enough time as tasks pile up...

a familiar struggle with stress many of us know. Fatigue and anxiety are hard to avoid.

Some days
I feel alone, not
wanting to be around
friends and family.
How can I find
the push to
get out there?

"This is all your fault"
"You are way too sensitive"
"I don't have to listen to you"
"I need to double-check everything you do"

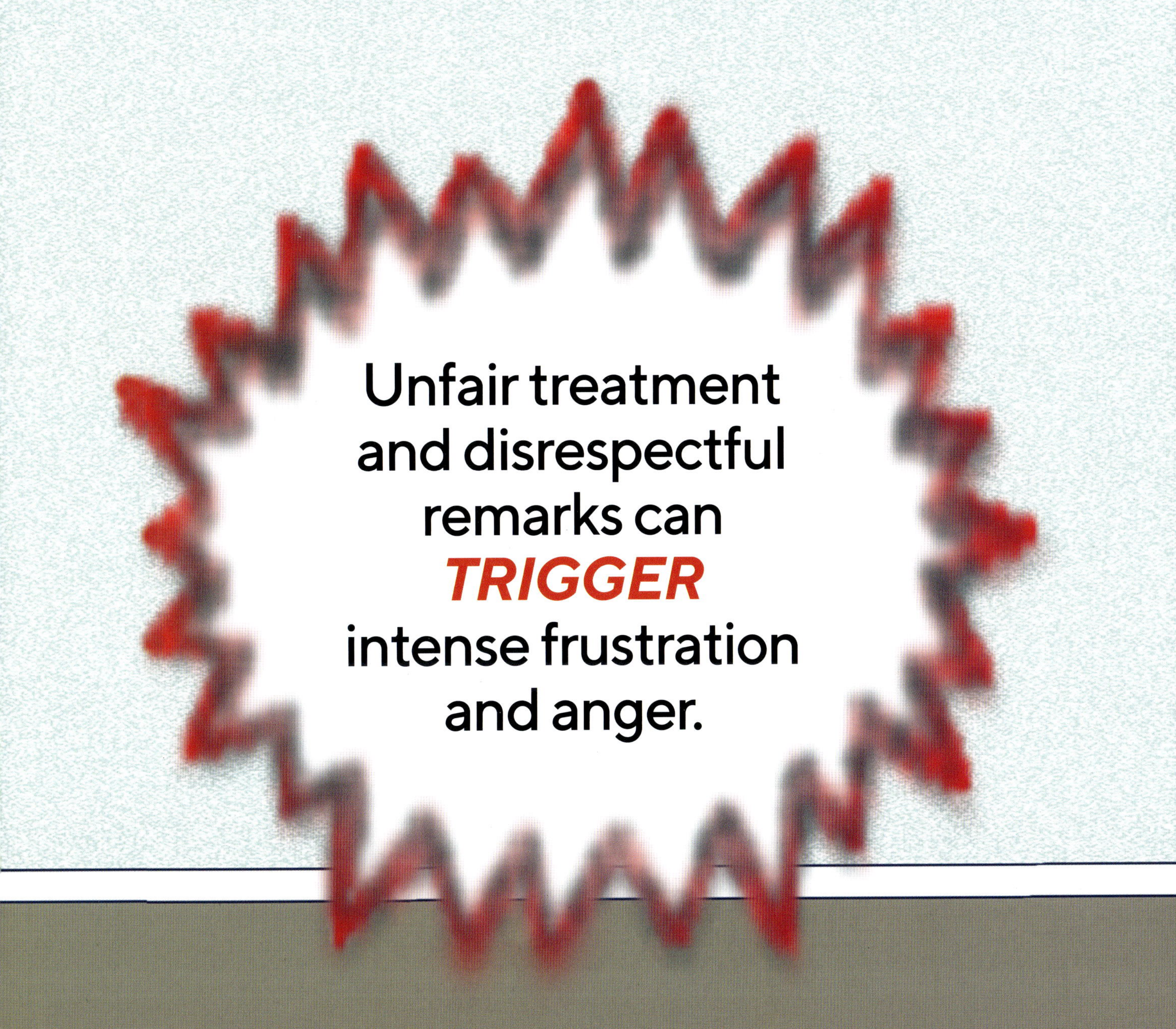
Unfair treatment
and disrespectful
remarks can
TRIGGER
intense frustration
and anger.

....I'm such a loser....
....It's all too hard....
....I give up....

There are moments when self-doubt and self-depreciation dominate.

Everything seems negative, mistakes glaring, lifestyle and relationships are questioned.

You deserve this
Well done!
YAY!

On some days
you are in your zone.
You achieve what you set out
to do, people acknowledge
what you've done.

These 'HIGHS' feel amazing.

Navigating lows can be tough. It can make us feel like we are **SPIRALLING OUT OF CONTROL**

You can feel like
you are stuck
in a black hole
with no way out.

TO DO
Exercise
Yoga
Practice Meditating
Healthier me!
Socialize
Contacts
Eat Better

Sunny is no stranger to trying different things to feel better and more in control.

You may question whether you can ride life's rollercoaster without freaking out.

IS THERE SOMETHING YOU CAN DO TO MAKE A LASTING CHANGE?

AHA!
LOOKOUT

The real game changer
for Sunny?
It's not outside forces.

IT'S THE WAY YOU SEE THE WORLD THAT TRANSFORMS EVERYTHING.

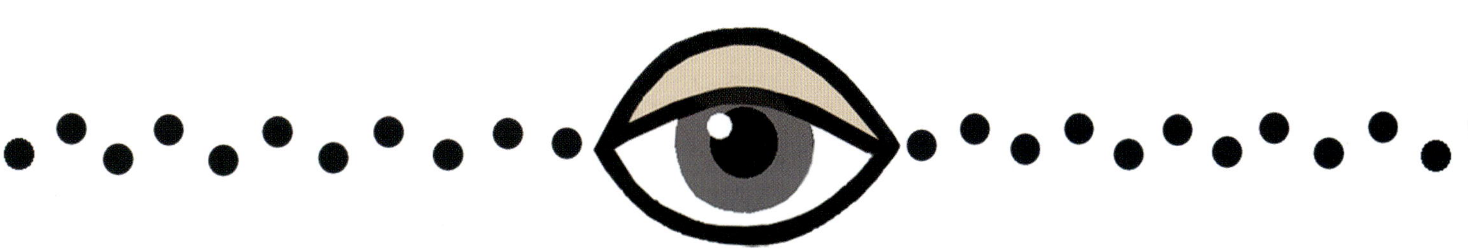

AHA! SCOPE

The
AHA! SCOPE
acts like a powerful lens
that helps your brain
see reality clearly,
free from negativity,
bias and distortion.

AHA!
AHA! SCOPE

AHA! MOMENTS

are sudden insights that clarify confusion. They change your thinking about stressful events.

Breakthroughs

happen when you harness energy from these moments.

BILLS
BILLS BILLS
BILLS
BILLS
BILLS
BILLS
In
Loving
Memory

BOTTLING UP STRESS CREATES INTERNAL PRESSURE.

Emotions need release through safe channels, like talking to trusted friends, journaling or seeking professional support.

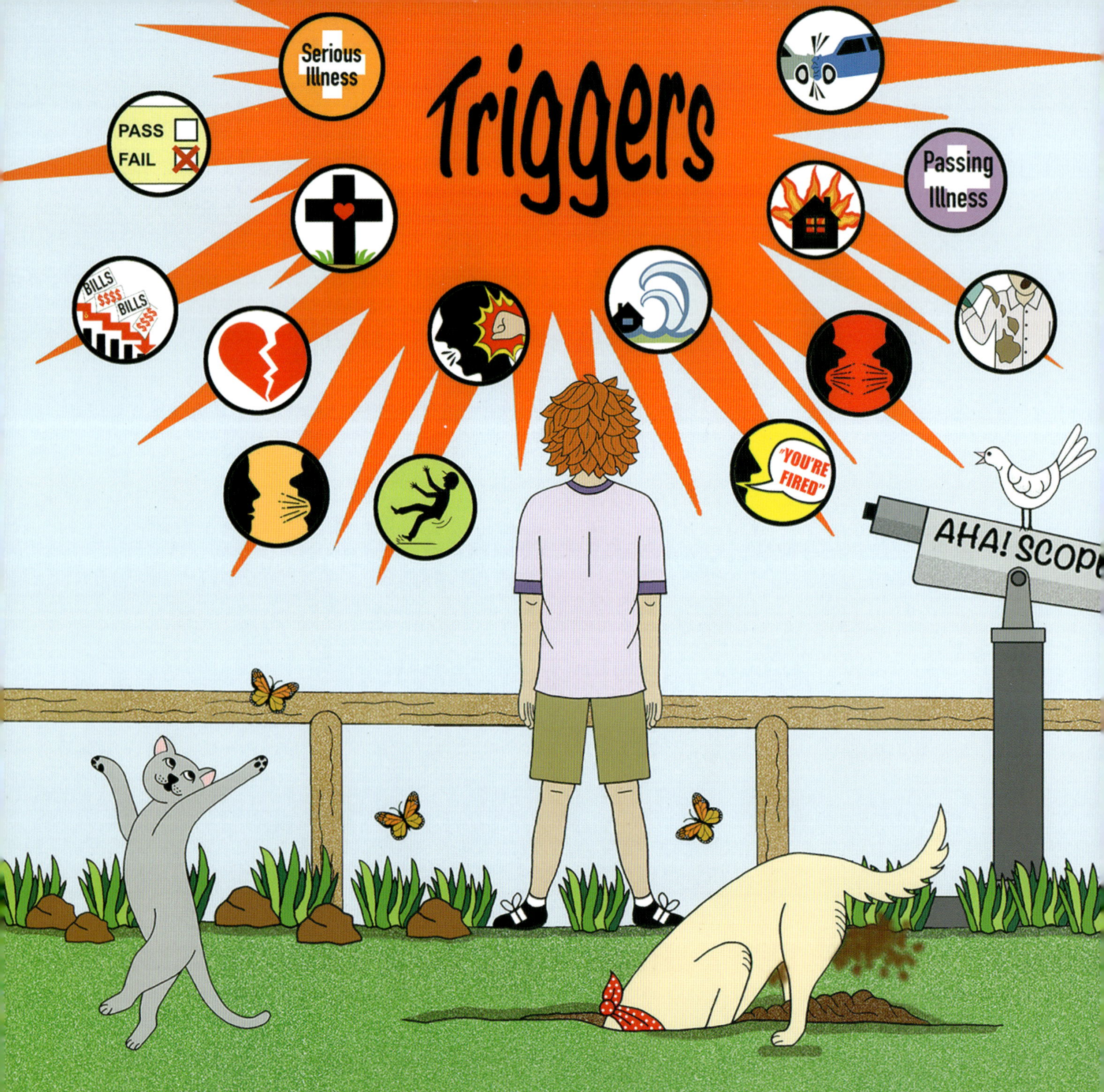
Triggers
Serious Illness
PASS
FAIL
Passing Illness
BILLS
$$$$
BILLS
$$$$
"YOU'RE FIRED"
AHA! SCOPE

It is helpful to become aware of your **TRIGGERS -** things such as memories, people and objects you are vulnerable to.

TRIGGERS CAN SPARK INTENSE NEGATIVE EMOTIONS.

EMOTIONAL
THERMOMETER
10+ intensely upset,
out of control
9
8 very upset,
7 losing control
6
moderately upset,
5 in control
4
3 a little upset
2
1 not upset at all
0

EMOTIONS HAVE TEMPERATURES, they aren't just ON or OFF.

Knowing the degree of emotional upset you experience helps you navigate stress and how difficult situations affect you.

NEGATIVE
THINKING
UNHELPFUL THOUGHTS

NEGATIVITY AND UNHELPFUL THOUGHTS WEIGH YOU DOWN.
AHA! SCOPE

This is awful
I can't
stand it
I'm a
LOSER
They're a
BASTARD
This isn't
the end
of the world
I accept
myself even when
I make mistakes
Doing the
wrong thing doesn't
mean someone is
totally bad

One of the most powerful AHA! Moments is this one...
YOU HAVE THE POWER TO CHANGE THE WAY YOU THINK.
Embracing this is life changing.
AHA! SCOPE

It's **NOT** your
parents, family,
friends, colleagues
or social media
that control the way you
see things and think.
IT'S YOU.

zzzZZZ

Z
Z
Z

Evicting the obnoxious roommate from your head helps you gain emotional control all day long and at night to sleep peacefully.

Z
Z
Z Z
Z

AHA! SCOPE

I'm a loser
No one listens to me
I should just give up
It's all too hard
I can't stand it
They don't like me
I just want to scream
They are horrible people

WHEN UPSET BY TRIGGERING EVENTS,
replace extreme thinking with thoughts that make sense.
AHA! SCOPE

Examining, writing down and replacing unhealthy thoughts with true, sensible ones can reduce emotional turmoil and promote positive, helpful behaviours.

Triggers

Extreme
Rigid
Not Sensible
Untrue

Moderate
Flexible
Sensible
Fact-based

Loss of Control

Intense Emotions

Self-defeating Actions

CONSEQUENCES

The Way You Feel & Behave

Self-control

Calmer Emotions

Goal-oriented Actions

THE ABC MODEL

shows that it's not the Adversity (A) that upsets you, but your Beliefs (B) about it that cause emotional and behavioural Consequences (C).

When you're very upset, check for extreme thoughts that are not sensible or true - and replace them with more balanced, realistic ones that make sense.

AHA! SCOPE

what it is......they all think I'm an idiot......is it really that bad?.....
an handle this..........no-one listens to....don't dwell in the past....
.........I should just give up..........I accept myself........life is awful..
n't stand this......I will ask for help......it's all my fault....I can fix i
..why me????....I failed but I learnt a lot.......I should be perfect...
ood....no-one's perfect......everyone is better than me.....I will try
othing goes right....I can find a way though this....always bad stu
give it my all, no matter what.....I always mess things up.....its al
ciate the good...I don't have any friends...I need to think about th
om bad to worse....at least I tried my best....I will never be a succ
ey are horrible people.....focus on the good things.......bad as it
.I can't control them but I can control me....they think I'm awful..
in the moment.....they make me so mad......think before reacting
..smile..........keep moving forward......they want to see me fail......
ey bring out the worst in me........I tried my best..........it's all my f
I need to focus on the positives....my thoughts are all negative...
THOUGHT CHECK

When you are feeling extremely upset, ask yourself,

"IS MY THINKING SENSIBLE, TRUE OR HELPFUL?"

If not, shift your thoughts to be less extreme and more helpful.

AHA! SCOPE

Me
Values
Personality
Experiences
Talents & Skills
Flaws
Family & Culture

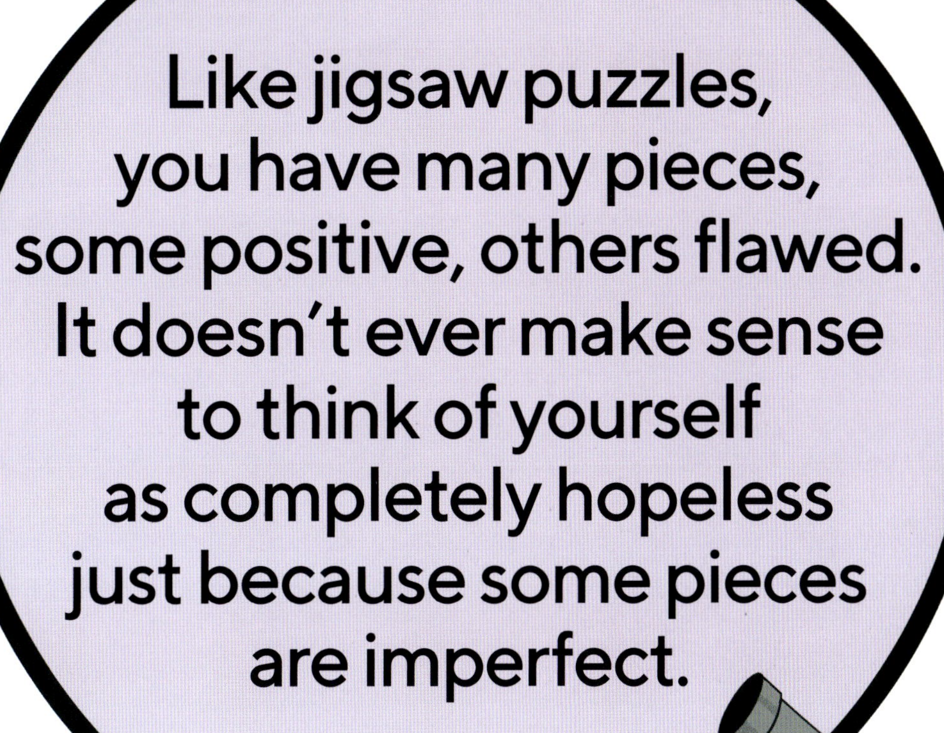

Like jigsaw puzzles,
you have many pieces,
some positive, others flawed.
It doesn't ever make sense
to think of yourself
as completely hopeless
just because some pieces
are imperfect.

That's not what I wanted you IDIOT

People have both positive and negative aspects. When they behave poorly, they are not entirely bad or useless.

THIS THINKING CREATES UNHEALTHY LEVELS OF ANGER.

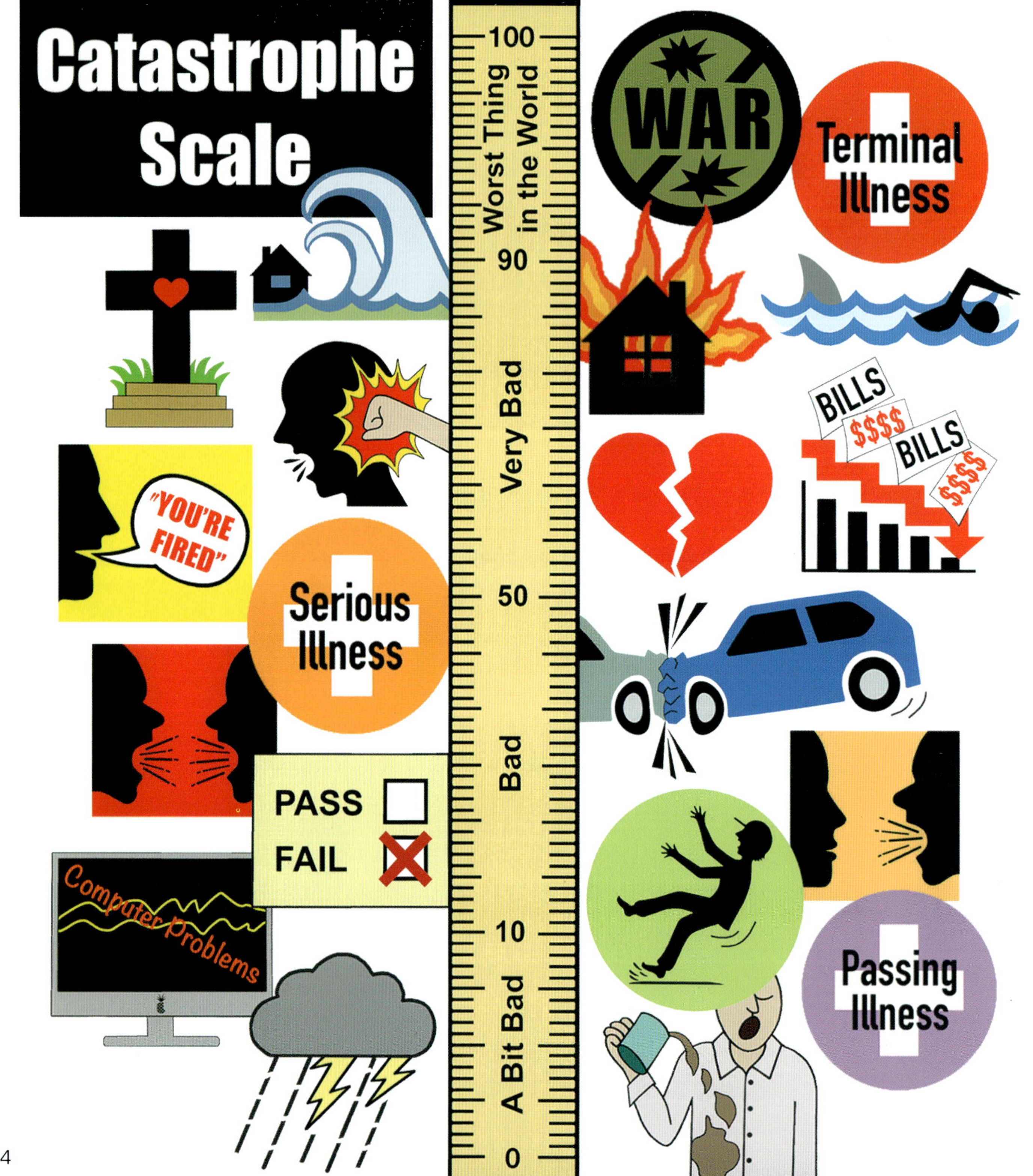
Catastrophe Scale
100
Worst Thing in the World
90
Very Bad
50
Bad
10
A Bit Bad
0
WAR
Terminal Illness
BILLS
$$$$
BILLS
$$$$
"YOU'RE FIRED"
Serious Illness
PASS
FAIL
Computer Problems
Passing Illness

CATASTROPHIC THINKING turns minor problems into disasters, accelerating anxiety. To regain control, ask yourself:

Who says I should?
I should be successful
I should be happy all the time
I should be perfect
I should always put others first

"SHOULDS"

exist only in your head and foster guilt and anxiety. Instead, say things to yourself like:

"I would prefer to, but don't have to,"

and

" I would like to but don't need to."

Aaaah...
I can't deal
with this
We must have
your report by
tomorrow

People with
"I-can't-stand-it-itis"
tend to exaggerate how
uncomfortable
something is.

They convince themselves
they can't handle
a situation – even when
they can.

AHA! SCOPE

I can't believe
your still at this.
I would have
given up
Yeah, I'm not
great at painting yet,
but I'm learning a lot
from just doing it!

A GROWTH MINDSET

fuels success and well-being. Regardless of age or experience, believe you can improve with effort and learning.

A FIXED MINDSET

limits growth by assuming improvement isn't possible.

What to DO

- take time out from stress
- do things you enjoy
- practice mindfulness, yoga
- find a trusted friend to talk with
- take stock of your positives
- accept yourself no matter what
- see the other person's point of view
- accept what you cannot change
- have the courage to change what you can
- speak to a mental health practitioner

When experiencing intense, unwanted emotions, best not to ignore them as they control you.

KNOWING WHAT TO DO AND WHAT NOT TO DO IS CRUCIAL.

THE WAY YOU SEE THE WORLD CAN HOLD YOU BACK OR SET YOU FREE -

- to explore new ventures
- to push yourself to take risks
- and to discover new aspects of yourself.

Take action when scared or unsure.
It will free you from emotional prison.
Accept that tolerating some discomfort is essential for personal growth.

You're
INVITED

ANXIETY OFTEN STEMS FROM WORRYING ABOUT OTHER PEOPLE'S OPINIONS.

While it's nice to be liked, it's okay if you're not liked all the time.

KEEP
GOING
PERSONAL
BEST
MOVING
FOWARD
PERFECTION

Now is not the time for perfection, just for moving forward.

Strive for your personal best but know you don't have to be perfect

NO ONE IS.

Seeing their luxury trips all over instagram makes me feel left behind
There's so much richness in life that doesn't come with a price tag. What gives you genuine joy?

When you get anxious
about missing out on
what others have,
**IT REALLY HELPS TO BE
GRATEFUL, CONTENT AND
FIND JOY IN WHAT
YOU HAVE.**

....I accept myself....
....No-ones perfect....
....I make mistakes....

To eliminate feeling very down when faced with a **TRIGGER** like criticism, someone being angry with you or unmet goals, Sunny avoids taking things personally. When you experience a trigger, tell yourself...

"I AM FINE BEING ME."

When you make mistakes and let yourself down, talk to yourself gently and with compassion.

TREAT YOURSELF WITH THE KINDNESS YOU'D OFFER A FRIEND IN THIS SITUATION.

When feeling low,
anxious or unmotivated,
do enjoyable activities
that uplift your mood
and shift your focus.

" This is your fault and now we all have to pay the price for your STUPIDITY "

Holding onto strong anger hurts yourself in the end.

When furious, you can say and do things you often later regret.

LET GO OF IT.

>>>ANGER MANAGEMENT SELF-TALK MENU<<<

"I can handle this calmly." *"It's OK to take a moment to breathe."*
"This feeling will pass. I don't need to act now."
"Don't condemn the sinner for the sin."
"I'm responsible for how I respond, not the other person's actions."
"I prefer, but don't need this person to do the right thing."

I've called for help

To keep frustration and anger under control when someone does something wrong, use reasonable and balanced self-talk.

POSITIVE SELF-TALK SHIFTS YOUR MINDSET AND DIFFUSES ANGER BEFORE ESCALATION.

It's
ME
time

To prevent burnout, create a routine that sets aside personal time, like walking, biking or closing your office door. Safeguard your energy by declining to do things that deplete you.

When stress hits hard,
be still and calm
in your mind.

**STAY GROUNDED
LIKE A ROCK**
and expansive like
the sky, unshaken by
whatever comes your way.

DO
DON'T STEW

Sunny now says

"NO TO PROCRASTINATION"

by thinking of the disadvantages of putting off things that need to be done and the benefits of getting things done **NOW**.

SUNNY
NO LONGER WAITS
FOR HAPPINESS.
Seek experiences
that bring joy and
fulfilment.

POSITIVE
THINKING
HELPFUL THOUGHTS

Face challenges with

OPTIMISM, POSITIVITY and HOPE.

I hate it that I can't dance anymore
I could dance all night but spending time with you is more important.

When looking for excitement, fun and new things to enjoy, make sure your happiness doesn't hurt family and friends who care about you.

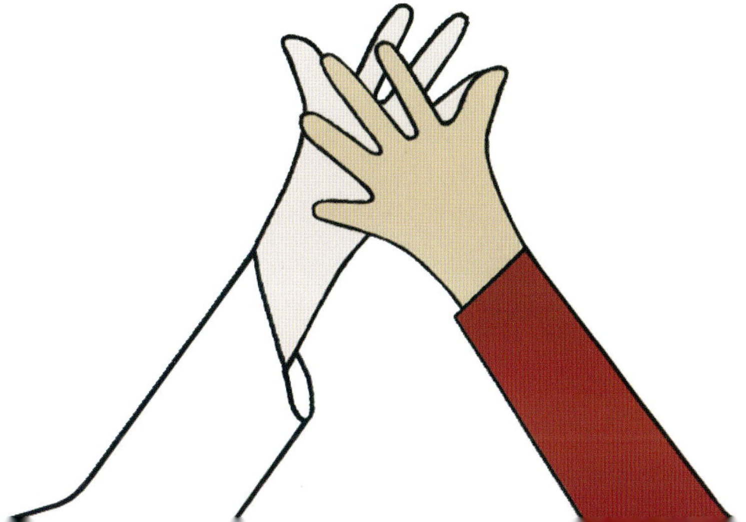

GIVE MORE TO RECEIVE MORE.

Healthy relationships are like vitamins for well-being and positive energy. Find micro-moments in your busy schedule to connect with people who uplift you.

I know what you all want but I just can't do it right now
Woof! Woof

Sunny shows
EMPATHY FOR OTHERS
by stepping into their shoes and thinking about the world from their point of view.

Listen and be understanding without having to agree, endorse or take action.

ACCEPT YOURSELF COMPLETELY.

Like a bowl of mixed fruit, we all have parts that are deliciously ripe, some overripe and some still maturing.

RESPECT
COURAGE
COMPASSION
CURIOSITY
HONESTY
GROWTH
ACTIONS DON'T REFLECT VALUES

KNOW YOUR VALUES BY REFLECTING ON WHAT TRULY MATTERS TO YOU.

Look at your daily actions and choices. Are they in line with what you believe matters most?

VALUES

AARGH!!
What should
I do?

DON'T FEAR DECISION-MAKING.

Aim for sound decisions. Accept that always being right is unrealistic.

HUMOUR ALLEVIATES STRESS.

Even during pain or overwhelming times, laughter helps. It's especially helpful to laugh at funny or absurd things, including your own mistakes.

CERTIFICATE OF
ACHIEVEMENT

Balance
your time
experiencing fun,
pleasure and excitement
with the hard work and
sacrifice needed to
to achieve your
longer term goals.

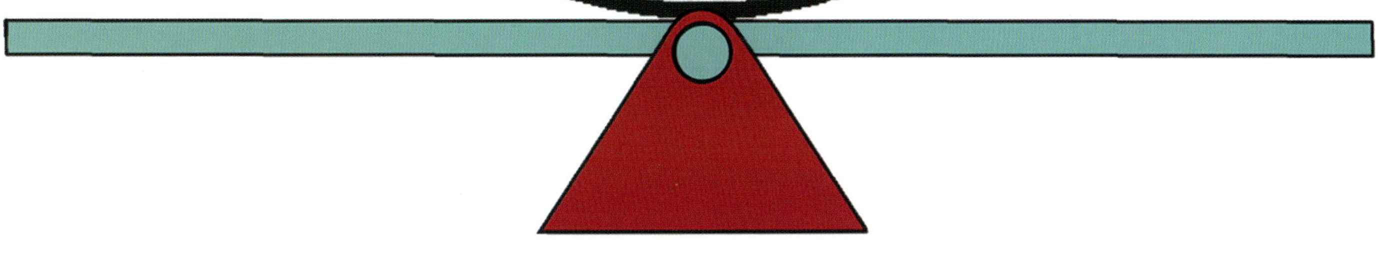

I LOVE your hat. It is soooo cool!

When you see someone excelling at a task or showcasing their individuality, make it a habit to appreciate and say something special about what you see.

Thank you for everything you've done

PRACTICE GRATITUDE
by taking the time to
express your appreciation.

Sunny is mindful
by being fully focused
on what's happening
in the present.
ENJOY THE MOMENT
without dwelling on
the past or worrying
about the future.

Have the serenity to accept the things you cannot change, the courage to change the things you can, and the wisdom to know the difference.

MAKE THESE AFFIRMATIONS PART OF YOUR DAILY LIFE, STARTING TODAY

Accept and be proud of who you are.

Happenings from the past do not define you, your choices do.

Assert yourself by doing what you love.

Make the most of and be grateful for what you have.

Our relationships succeed by accepting, not judging anyone.

Mindfulness is spending time in the present moment.

Everyday, find the courage to take values-driven action.

Negative inner dialogues that weigh you down can be evicted.

Triggers can be managed with helpful rather than unhelpful thoughts.

Set yourself free by taking risks and exploring new aspects of yourself.

THANKS TO AHA! MOMENTS,

Sunny no longer freaks out in 'bad weather', actively embracing life and dealing positively with challenges.

Your destiny lies
within, not in the stars.
The way you see
the world shapes reality.
You are who you are and
and where you are
because of
YOU!

NOTES

NOTES

AHA! SCOPE